LAW IS
NOT OF FAITH

LAW IS
NOT OF FAITH
WHAT MOST PREACHERS DON'T WANT YOU TO KNOW

M. AVERIAL OWENS

Xulon Press

Xulon Press
2301 Lucien Way #415
Maitland, FL 32751
407.339.4217
www.xulonpress.com

Unless otherwise indicated, Scripture quotations taken from the New American Standard Bible (NASB). Copyright © 1960, 1962, 1963, 1968, 1971, 1972, 1973, 1975, 1977, 1995 by The Lockman Foundation. Used by permission. All rights reserved.

Scripture quotations taken from the King James Version (KJV)–*public domain*.

Printed in the United States of America.

ISBN-13: 978-1-6322-1943-5
Ebook: 978-1-6322-1944-2

Dedication

I want to dedicate this book to the late Pastor Bob George. It was through his radio ministry called "People to People" that I received much of this revelation knowledge. It was so enlightening and profound that I decided to write this book to help other believers find the truth about the New Covenant. And to my lovely wife Sara, for her love, support, and encouragement.

Table of Contents

FOREWORD

I'm going to tell you something that **MOST** preachers don't want you to know. They do not want you to know that you are not under Old Covenant **tithe law**! Did that get your attention? You are not "_cursed with a curse_" if you don't give ten percent of your income to a preacher. That curse was directed to the **_nation of Israel_** under the Old Covenant of Law in the book of Malachi, over 400 years _before_ the birth of Jesus. There were no Christians at the time the book of Malachi was written, so it doesn't even apply to Christians. If you will allow me, I will demonstrate in the following chapters how we have been misled and deceived by _most_ modern-day preachers. Not only about tithing but about **_many_** other things. Trust me, the _world_, the _flesh_, and the _devil_ do not want you to know what I am about to reveal to you in this book. Pay close attention to what happens when you start studying this book. Your phone will start ringing, your doorbell will sound, and all kinds of interruptions will begin to happen. That's the world, the flesh, and the devil calling. Trying as hard as it can to hinder you from finding out about the truth regarding the New Covenant of Jesus Christ.

The apostle Paul in the New Covenant said, "Each one must do(or give) just as he has purposed in his heart, **_not_** grudgingly or **_under compulsion_**, for God loves a cheerful giver." (2 Cor. 9:7). We are not under compulsion to give. The definition of compulsion is, "the action or state of forcing or _being forced_ to do something." No one is cheerful when coerced to do something. This new teaching on giving by the apostle Paul completely contradicts the tithe law, which was given under the Old Covenant. This contradiction confuses modern-day believers and we need to address it. This Old Covenant law of tithing is pounded into our brains over and over again in most churches or (brick buildings I call them) almost every other Sunday, more than any other teaching. The **real church** is the body of Christ, the born-again believers called the _ecclesia_—not the

2

brick buildings. We hear it so often, to the point that we have become brain-washed into zombie-like behavior. They try their best to scare us into surrendering a per-centage of our income to them, these preachers (these lawyers-of-religion), for *fear* of being under a curse. And lawyers are good at finding *loopholes* in the *law*. The problem is, that we as New Covenant believers are *not under* Old Covenant Law, and that includes the **tithe** *law*! "For God has not given us a *spirit of fear*; but of power, and of love, and of a sound mind." (2 Tim. 1:7).

We are under a New Covenant of grace. Most preachers do not want you to know that because that would derail their gravy train. Law and grace are like **oil and water**; they don't mix. They are complete oppo-sites, which *contradict and nullify* one another. But, most believers cannot tell the difference because of all of the false and *out of context* teachings they've been subjected to. These lawyers of religion have taken full advantage of this biblical *confusion*, to turn their brick and mortar buildings into money-making businesses. They are trying to turn the **sheep** into **milk cows**. Jesus said to *feed* my sheep, not to *fleece* **my** sheep. I don't believe this is what Lord Jesus had in mind for His fol-lowers. As I remember reading, He drove out the money changers in the temple for making a *profit* off the worshippers. Not only about tithing, but I intend to expose several other *out of context* and false teachings being perpetrated by our modern-day *lawyers of religion*.

"For the **love of money** is a root of all sorts of evil, and some by longing for it have wandered away from the faith" (1 Tim. 6:10). Jesus taught that we should give to the **poor**, to the **orphans** and **widows**, and by doing so we would be *storing up treasure* in heaven. The apostle Paul later added that we should also give to anyone who **ministers Truth**. If a preacher is teaching that you are under Old Covenant Law, such as the tithe law, he is not ministering truth. So why should you give your hard-earned money to someone who is *deceiving you*? This false and *out of context* teaching is only one of many I have discovered in the past fifty years of my Christian experience. I will uncover more for you in the following chapters. I will show you where to find the scriptures in God's word that will prove I am teaching **truth** in the **proper context**. *Truths* or *half-truths* taught *out of context,* is not the truth, but **a lie**.

I am writing this book mainly for my fellow believers in Christ Jesus, in order to help them understand how to properly discern the stark difference between Law and grace. Once you have a more clear understanding of this New Covenant of Grace that we Christians have entered into with God, you will feel as though you have been **born-again again**, and you will begin to feel the freedom and joy that you experienced when you first came to faith in Lord Jesus. And this time the feeling will never leave you, because it's the _real_ good news that most preachers do not teach. It will always be just under the surface of your spirit, ready to resurface and bubble up into *effervescent joy,* every time you hear the mere mention of the wonderful name of Jesus. Blessed be His name!

The apostle Paul said many times, that believers in Lord Jesus are not under Law but under Grace. Here's one example, "For sin shall not be master over you, for you are **not under law** but under grace" (Rom. 6:14). He also said that, "_All things_ are lawful, but not all things are profitable" (1 Cor. 10:23). Simply put, the power of sin is in the law and if you are not under law **sin has no power** over you, meaning sin can no longer cause you _spiritual death_ once you are born-again. The **New Covenant** only gets better and better, the more you learn about it!

If you have an open mind and are still teachable (*humble*), God will give you grace (*undeserved favor*), and will reveal and confirm to your spirit by His Holy Spirit, revelation knowledge of the New Covenant scriptures mentioned in this book. "God resists the proud but gives grace to the humble" (James 4:6). Once the Holy Spirit confirms these truths to your spirit, the chains of bondage to religious tradition and *out of context* teaching will begin to *loosen and fall off*, one by one, setting you free, *never to be in bondage* to them again!

If you're seeking truth, **I've found what you're looking for** in the New Covenant of Messiah Jesus. Notice, I didn't say the New Testament, there is a good reason for it. I will go into more detail about that in a later chapter. Truth is not easy to find. The Word of God is like a *giant puzzle* that spans over a period of thousands of years, and has many interlocking pieces of **eternal truths**. Through this teaching you will discover that when covenants change, **spiritual truths** can change too. And like most puzzles, you never see the big picture until all the pieces have come together.

I challenge you not to take this teaching at face value. Search out the context of the scriptures listed in this book in your own Bible. By doing so, you will find out for yourself which scriptures are in the Old Covenant of Law and which are in the New Covenant of grace. Once I show you how to discern the context of scripture, you will realize that you have finally found the truth you've been searching for. Don't feel bad. You are not alone. It took me thirty-two years of going to the *brick buildings* before I found the *truth* about the New Covenant. And I didn't find it there. I found it listening to a preacher on the radio who was not trying to get money out of me. Once you learn the ***truth*** you must hold onto it like a ***pit bulldog***. Because the **world**, the **flesh**, and the **devil** do not want you to find this **truth**.

You may notice that I will mention some bible verses and some important phrases in more than one chapter. Remember, I told you it's like a giant puzzle and some-times one verse of scripture touches or interconnects with others to make a complete picture. If you've been taught something correctly the first time you hear it, you may only need to hear it five or six more times before you ***internalize*** it. However, if you've been taught something incorrectly, it may take hearing it over and over again the correct way forty or fifty times before you finally ***get it***! In other words you may have to **unlearn** much of the *out of context* teaching you have been subjected to for so many years before you are able to internalize it in the correct context. To understand **truth** in the correct context, you must see God's word through the *lens* of the New Covenant. *Any man* can tell you what scripture says, but only the Holy Spirit can reveal the '***meaning***' to your spirit.

"For the one who has entered ***His*** rest has himself also ***rested from his works***, as God did from ***His***" (Hebrews 4:10). And "But if it is by grace, it is *no longer on the basis of works*, otherwise *grace is no longer grace*" (Romans 11:6). By internalizing the teachings in this book, you will learn how to ***rest from your own works,*** striving to be righteous in the eyes of God, by trying to keep Old Covenant Law. And instead, learn how to ***enter His rest*** through *saving faith* in the finished work of Lord Jesus and His New Covenant of Grace. Only then will you find "the peace of God which surpasses all comprehension, will guard your hearts and your minds in Christ Jesus" (Phil. 4:7).

CHAPTER 1

THE TRUTH WILL MAKE YOU FREE

W hat is **Truth**? Jesus said, "I am the *way*, the *truth*, and the *life*; no one comes to the Father, but through Me" (John 14:6). Jesus is the **Truth**. Now, if we can all agree on that, let's continue. Christian scholars, who can translate the ancient Greek and ancient Hebrew languages, claim that the **NASB** (New American Standard Bible) first published in 1901 as the **ASB** (American Standard Bible), is the most accurate translation of the ancient manuscripts. The New

International Version (NIV) is second to that. I can't read ancient Hebrew or ancient Greek, so I will have to trust the scholar's judgement in this matter. I highly recommend that if you are seeking ***truth***, that you get a copy of each of these two versions of the Bible. After studying and comparing many different translations of the Bible, I've found these two versions to be the most accurate.

As a young believer, I studied the Old King James Bible first printed in 1611. Later, I found that it had incorrectly translated some verses. These are now corrected in the printing of the _New_ King James Bible. One inaccurate translation of a Bible verse I found was in the Book of Exodus in the _Old_ King James version. Where it lists the Ten Commandments. One of which is, "***Thou shalt not kill***" (Exod. 20:13). But, now in the _New_ King James version the same verse says, "***You shall not murder***." This is what the more accurate versions of the Bible say. There is a big difference between ***kill*** and ***murder***. You may have to ***kill*** in self-defense, or go to war to fight for your country. But the definition of ***murder*** is ***killing of the innocent*** or _without just cause_, such as ***murdering*** a baby in its mother's womb.

Jesus said in (John 8:32), "you will know the truth, and the truth will make you free." If _truth makes you_ *free*, then it stands to reason that *error puts you in bondage*. These days, many believers are in bondage to preconceived ideas, religious traditions, and to *out of context* teachings of the Bible. Many *believers* are **still in bondage** to the Old Covenant of Law which was first given by God to Moses on Mt. Sinai. It began with the Ten Commandments. Then, followed by *hundreds* of other laws and commandments in the *Torah* (Book of the Law), which consists of the *first five* books of the Old Testament.

The New Covenant of Grace was ushered in when Lord Jesus shed His blood on the cross, paying for the sins of the *world*. He rendered the Old Covenant of Law obsolete. "When He said, "A new covenant, He has made the first **obsolete**." (Heb. 8:13) The definition of obsolete is; *no longer used or produced*, out of date, **invalid**! The words *covenant*, *testament*, and *will* are all interchangeable, and have the same meaning. As we know, a **will** does not go into *force* until the one who made it dies. In the same manner, the New Covenant of Grace *did not go into effect* **until Jesus died** on the cross. The scripture that supports this truth is found in the New Covenant, which is *after the crucifixion* of Christ. "For where a *covenant* is, there must of necessity be the *death* of the one who made it. For a covenant is *valid* only when *men are dead*, for it is *never in force* while the *one who made it lives*" (Hebrews 9:16-17). This is the *key* verse in understanding where to **rightly divide** the **word of truth**. It shows *exactly* where the Old Covenant of **Law ends**, and where the New Covenant of **Grace begins**; at the Cross. Without a proper understanding of this scripture, many verses in the Bible will seem contradictory and confusing. More than likely you've probably never been taught the *truth* about this passage of scripture before by any preacher at any time. Honestly, in the past fifty years of my Christian experience I've only heard one preacher teach on it myself. And once I understood what it meant, it completely opened my eyes and changed me from being a *religious person* into a *spiritual believer*!

This new understanding helps clear up the confusion and what appears as *contradictions* in the scriptures. For example, Jesus said, "**If you do not forgive** others, then your **Father will not forgive** your transgressions" (Matt. 6-15). Jesus taught this while He was still alive, under the Old Covenant of Law. Remember, the New Covenant did not go into force until His death. Jesus had to *keep the Law* **under the Old Covenant** to be a worthy sacrifice

12

for the world's sin. This teaching of Jesus (*under the law*) that *forgiveness was conditional*, and that God will not forgive you unless you forgive others, *contradicts* what is taught in the New Covenant. Compare it to what the apostle Paul said *after the crucifixion*, "God was in Christ reconciling the **world** to Himself, *not counting their trespasses* against them" (2 Cor. 5:19). Did you catch that? Let me break it down for you. After the crucifixion, God said He is **not counting our trespasses** (sins) against us. Which is true, (Matt. 6:15) or (2 Cor. 5:19)? The answer is that they were *both true at the time they were given*. But, they were each given under a **different covenant**! (Matt. 16:5) was given under the Old Covenant of Law (before Jesus died), and (2 Cor. 5:19) was given under the New Covenant of Grace(after Jesus died). What happened? Something changed— **Jesus had been crucified**! The penalty for sin was paid. Forgiveness is now offered to us without condition, and the New Covenant was **now in force**. I agree with the idea that *we should forgive* others. Otherwise, a root of bitterness will grow in our spirit and will affect all aspects of our life. However, to **not forgive** *is not the unforgivable sin* under the New Covenant of Grace as *Jesus* said it was under the Old Covenant of Law! The

New Testament begins with the Book of Matthew, but the _New Covenant_ does not begin until the Book of Acts—after the death of Jesus!

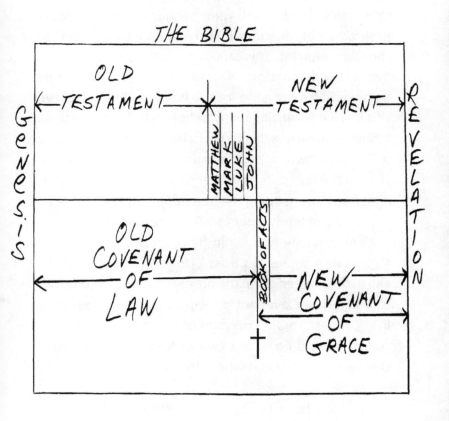

Sadly, there are very few modern-day preachers who rightly divide the *word of truth* for their congregations. Some teach parts of the New Covenant (the parts that don't conflict with their agenda or their building program), but then they mix in contradictory aspects of the Old Covenant. This causes confusion, guilt, and feelings of condemnation. Whether this is by design or by ignorance, it's not good for the Body of Christ. I believe this is what is causing many believers to leave the brick buildings in droves. If you try to mix Law and grace, you will end up with a big confusing mess. And we know who scripture calls the author of confusion, Satan. Again, comprehending the '*meaning*' of (Hebrews 9:16-17) can completely clear up all this confusion.

"For the Law was given by Moses, but *grace* and *truth* came by Jesus Christ" (John 1:17). During His short three-year ministry on earth, Jesus attempted to teach New Covenant principles to Jewish followers living under the Old Covenant of Law. Sometimes Jesus compared Old Covenant Law to New Covenant Truth. One example of this is where He said,

> "You have heard that it was said,'*You shall not commit adultery*'; but I say to you that everyone who *looks at a woman with lust* for her has already **committed adultery** with her **in his**

heart" (Matt. 5:27-28). Another example is where Jesus said, "You have heard that the ancients were told, **'You shall not commit murder'** and 'Whoever commits murder shall be liable to the court.' But I say to you that everyone who is **angry with his brother** shall be *guilty* before the court" (Matt. 5:21-22).

In other words, **guilty of murder** in his heart! The Law deals with the *flesh*, but the New Covenant *raises the bar higher* and goes deeper, dealing with the very *spirit* of man. We have all committed adultery and murder in our hearts(in our spirit). And God looks at the heart. "God sees not as man sees, for man looks at the outward appearance, but the **Lord looks at the heart**" (1 Sam.16:7). These are only a couple of examples of the difference between Law and Grace, there are many more. At one point the apostles asked Jesus,

"Then who can be saved?" And looking at them Jesus said to them, "With people this is impossible, but with God all things are possible" (Matt. 19:25-26).

"Salvation belongs to the **_Lord_**" (Ps. 3:8).
Jesus said, "God is spirit, and those who
worship Him must worship in _spirit and
in truth_" (John 4:24).

In other words, we must be honest and truthful with
God **_in our spirit_** even though our flesh is not always
obedient to Him. Remember, God looks at the **heart**
(_your spirit_).

"All scripture is inspired by God and is profitable for
teaching, for reproof, for correction, for training in righteousness; so that the man of God may be adequate,
equipped for every good work" (2 Tim. 3:16). This is
true, but to find the _truth in context_, we should view the
Old Covenant _through the lens_ of the New Covenant. If
an Old Covenant _Law_ contradicts a New Covenant _truth_,
we must **_reject_** the Old for the New or we will become
confused and feel condemned. "Therefore there is now
no condemnation for those who are in Christ Jesus.
For the **_law_** of the **Spirit of Life** in Christ Jesus has **set
you free** from the **law of sin and death**" (Rom. 8:1-2).
The Spirit of life is the Holy Spirit, and He dwells in the
believer, setting us free from condemnation and the

curse of the law of sin and death. Hallelujah, thank you Holy Spirit!

"But now He(Jesus), has obtained a more excellent ministry, by as much as He is also the ***mediator* of a better covenant**, which has been enacted on ***better promises***" (Heb. 8:6). "Study to show yourself approved to God as a workman who does not need to be ashamed, ***rightly dividing/accurately handling*** the word of truth" (2 Tim.2:15). You see, there is a dividing line in the Word of God between the Old Covenant of Law and the New Covenant of Grace. There are also different contexts within the New Covenant that need to be understood to avoid confusion. The apostle Paul wrote almost *two-thirds* of the New Testament. At times he was speaking to believers, and at other times to, or about unbelievers. Without realizing this, some passages of scripture even in the New Covenant, can cause you to feel guilt and condemnation. But remember, the word says, "there is now **no condemnation** for those who are in Christ" (Rom. 8:1). If you feel this way while reading scripture from the New Covenant, you probably are not under-standing the ***context*** of what you are reading.

"The wages of sin is death, but the ***free* gift** of God is ***eternal* life** in Christ Jesus our Lord" (Rom. 6:23). Did you notice the words *free gift* and *eternal life*? Free means you (didn't earn it) or have to (work for it), and eternal means **forever**. "For by **grace** you have been saved **through faith**; and that not of yourselves, it is the **gift** of God; *not as a result of works* (doing good deeds or trying to keep the law), so that no one may boast" (Eph. 2:8-9). Again, grace means (unmerited favor). Through faith,(**faith in Jesus and His works—not faith in our works**). Did you get that? Jesus must be the *object* of our faith, not our *effort in futility* in the energy of our flesh of trying to keep the Law. Jesus was living during the time the Old Covenant was in force (before the cross). He had to keep *all the laws—all the time* to be a worthy **sacrificial lamb** without spot or blemish, which is something we cannot do. He was the righteous one who merited God's favor, not us—we're sinners. We must learn to depend totally on Him and His works, not only to save us but to make us righteous before a Holy God. "But we are **all** as an unclean thing, and **all** our righteousnesses are as **_filthy rags_**" (Isa. 64:6). We have **no righteousness** (right standing with God) apart from Him and His Holy Spirit. "He made **_Him who knew no sin_**, to be sin on our behalf, so that we might become the **_righteousness of God_** in Him" (2 Cor 5:21).

Jesus said, "Enter through the *narrow gate*; for the gate is wide and the way is broad that leads to destruction, and there are many who enter through it. For the gate is small and the way is narrow that leads to *Life*, and there are *few* who find it" (Matt. 7:13-14). If you are seeking truth, start looking at the Word of God *through the lens* of the New Covenant of Grace. You will see the Word of God in a whole new light as you have never seen it before. Grace **supercedes** Law after the cross in the New Covenant. I tell you the truth, you must be born-again to see the kingdom of heaven, and you must enter in through the *narrow gate* of Christ Jesus and His New Covenant of Grace.

No one entered heaven in the Old Testament under the Covenant of Law, not even Abraham or Moses, even though they had faith. Their faith was credited to them as righteousness, not their works of trying to keep the law. All the Old Testament believers were *sinners* too, every one of them! (Rom. 4:3) states, "Abraham believed God, and it was credited to him as righteousness." Under the Old Covenant of Law, the spirits of those who died and had faith in God went to a holding place called **Abraham's bosom**. Yes, they called it Paradise, but it was not heaven. They were being held

21

captive there, waiting for the Messiah that would come after dying on the cross to pay for their sins, before they could gain access to heaven. After the death of Jesus, it says, "When He ascended on high, He led *captive a host of* **captives**, and He gave gifts to men" (Eph. 4:8). Here, it's referring to Jesus, after He died on the cross and was resurrected, going to Abraham's bosom where He preached the good news to the Old Testament believers who were being held captive. And to all *who believed* He took with Him to heaven. Jesus said, "**Repent and believe in the gospel**" (Mark 1:15). We can all enter heaven now bypassing Abraham's bosom, through the New Covenant of Grace in Jesus Christ—*the narrow gate*, if we repent of our **sin of unbelief** and believe.

CHAPTER 2

THE
SALVATION PUZZLE

W hat is the meaning of <u>*SALVATION*</u>? In my opinion, each one of us needs to know the correct answer to this important question before leaving this world and stepping out into eternity. Each and every one of us has an appointment with physical death, some much sooner than others. The mystery of salvation is not complicated but it is complex, and yet it takes a ***child-like faith*** to find it. The disciples asked Jesus, "Who then is greatest in the kingdom of heaven?" And He called a child to Himself and set him before them, and said, "Truly I say to you, unless you are ***converted*** and ***become like children***, you will not enter the kingdom of heaven. Whoever then *humbles himself* as this child, he is the greatest in the kingdom of heaven" (Matt.18:2-4). The definition of humble is having a modest or low estimate of one's own importance; not proud or haughty, and ***remaining teachable***.

> "God is *opposed* to the proud, but gives grace to the humble. Submit therefore to God. Resist the devil and he will flee from you. Draw near to God and He will draw near to you. Cleanse your hands, you sinners; and purify your hearts, you double-minded. Humble yourselves in the presence of the Lord, and He will exalt you" (James 4:6-8,10).

According to God's divine purpose He slowly revealed the mystery of His plan of salvation, like a *giant puzzle* piece by piece, over a period of thousands of years through His prophets who hoped that they would see the day of the coming Messiah. Throughout the sixty-six books of the Bible written by around forty different authors, including the prophets who gave over *one hundred prophecies* about the coming Messiah, which were *all fulfilled* and ultimately culminated in the person of Christ Jesus.

In this chapter, I will be putting pieces of the puzzle together for you, so you can see the big picture of what true salvation is and how it is personally realized. As I said before, any man can tell you what scripture says, but the '*meaning*' of scripture has to be revealed to your spirit by the Holy Spirit. Jesus said in (John 3:3), "Truly, truly, I say to you, unless one is **born-again**, he cannot see the kingdom of God." The Word of God says we have a choice to make as to where we will spend eternity after our physical body dies, either in heaven or hell. Heaven being described as a place called paradise, where there is, "no more death, no sorrow, nor crying, neither shall there be any more pain;(Rev. 21:4). Jesus described **Hell** as the **Outer Darkness**, being separated from God, "where there will be **weeping and gnashing** of teeth" (Luke 13:28). The book of Revelation states that at the end of the age, after the 7-year tribulation period, those who are in the outer darkness, will be thrown in to a **Lake of Fire**, prepared for the devil who

25

deceived them, where their worm dieth not and the fire is not quenched and they will be **tormented** *day and night* forever and ever." (Rev. 20:10 & Mark 9:44). God has given you free will, which one will you choose? If you decide not to choose, you still have *made a choice*! (Deut. 30:19) states, "I call heaven and earth to witness against you today, that I have set before you, **_life_** *and* **_death_**, the *blessing* and the *curse*. **_Choose life_** in order that you may live, you and your descendants."

In (Matt 7:7-8) Jesus said, "Ask, and it will be given unto you; knock, and it will be opened to you. For *everyone* that asks receives, and he who seeks finds, and to him who knocks it will be opened." God will not force you to believe. You must ask, seek and knock. "You will seek Me and find Me when you search for Me with **_all your heart_**" (Jer. 29:13). In (Heb. 11:6) we find, "Without faith it is impossible to please God, for he who comes to God must believe that **He is** (God) and that He is a rewarder of those who *diligently* seek Him. God will reward you with salvation, of being **born-again**, if you *diligently* seek Him.

I've found that most people, *even believers* do not fully understand what is meant by the term "**born-again**." In most cases, no one has really broken it down for them as to how salvation is achieved according to the Word of God. When asked some respond by saying, "you have to be a good person, or you have to repent, or you must keep asking God to forgive you." Many even say you have to continue **striving** to _keep the Law_! However good these answers or intentions seem to be, they cannot in and of themselves guarantee you the free gift of eternal life, of being born-again. Have you heard the old adage, "The road to hell is paved with good intentions?" It's probably true! Nobody's perfect, we are all sinners. As for trying to be a **good-person**, according to the Word of God no one can be good enough to earn their way into heaven. It's too late, we've already sinned, and even if we hadn't we were _born in sin_ because of our ancestors Adam and Eve's original sin. Secondly, how can we say we've _repented_ when we continue committing the very same sins **_over and over_** again? Isn't that something unbelievers would use to accuse us of being a _hypocrite_? Of course they would, if they found out about it! They love to call us Christians _hypocrites._ Even though they don't even try to improve their own behavior. They gladly rush to judge and condemn us when we stumble or make a mistake.

In biblical times, the word *repent* had a very strict meaning, which was doing a 180-degree about-face, and going in the opposite direction never to repeat that same sin again. By having to ask God *to forgive us* over and over again only proves that we have not repented, because we keep committing the same sins. And **striving** *to keep the Law* is an effort in futility, because *you* would have to keep *all the laws-all the time* in order to be made righteous by your works. That's called works righteousness, and as I've said before you can't be "good enough" to work your way into heaven. (Ephesians 2:8-9) explains this very clearly, "For by grace you have been saved through faith; and that not of yourselves, it is the gift of God; *not as a result of works*, so that no one may boast."

Your good works don't save you, and your good works don't keep you saved. Only Lord Jesus kept all of God's laws perfectly, and that's what it would require for you to be made righteous in the eyes of God. It's your faith in *His* works (Jesus's works) that saves you, not your faith in your works! This is something I've found that most believers do not understand. Let me *break-it-down* for you, we are saved by **grace** (God's favor which we don't deserve—because we're sinners), through *faith* (faith in His Son Jesus—the One who does deserve God's favor), and *not as a result of our works* (our effort in futility of striving to keep all of God's laws—all the time). We can't do it and we don't do it, no matter how much we want to or how hard we try. Which is made evident by our frequently having to ask God to forgive us. That's what Jesus was talking about when He said, "The *spirit is willing*, but the *flesh is weak*" (Matt. 26:41). Our flesh cannot keep God's laws all the time, especially in this fallen world! We can't even keep the first Ten Commandments all the time, much less all the other 1653 laws and commandments listed in the Old and New Testaments combined. If we could, we wouldn't need Jesus to get us into heaven, we could get there on our own!

The old Rabbi *Nicodemus* asked Jesus, "How can a man be born-again when he is old? He cannot enter a second time into his mother's womb and be born, can he?" Jesus answered, "Truly, truly, I say to you, unless one is born of water and the Spirit he cannot enter into the kingdom of God. That which is born of the *flesh is flesh*, and that which is born of the *Spirit* is *spirit*. Do not be amazed that I said to you, you must be born-again" (John 3:5-7).

Let's search the scriptures to find other pieces of the puzzle in order to understand what Jesus meant by the term "born-again." The Bible says, "The next day John the Baptist saw Jesus coming to him and said, "Behold the lamb of God who *takes away the sin of the **world***" (John 1:29). This verse is very important as it describes one of the very important works Jesus accomplished by His death on the cross. It states that the sin of the **world** was taken away by the shedding of His blood on the cross for mankind (not just the sin of believers). We were **all** *forgiven* at the cross, both *believers* and *unbelievers*. Yes, whether one chooses to believe it or not, that's what happened. I know what (1 John 1:9) says, and I will prove to you that this is another verse that preachers have twisted and taught out of context, because it *fits their agenda*. We will do a more in-depth study in a later chapter about the proper context of (1 John 1:9). Just trust me for now that they've also been teaching that *out of context*. Jesus paid for the sins of the world, past, present, and future sins, without us having to *constantly ask Him* for it. "Let God be found true, though every man be found a liar, as it is written" (Rom. 3:4).

Think about it, when Jesus died to pay for the sins of the world, it was about 2,000 years before you were born! When Jesus died and paid for your sin, *all your sins were in the future*, because you had not been born yet! That's right, He paid for your future *sins* as well as for the future sins of the world. We were all born forgiven, but we were born **spiritually DEAD**! That's why Lord Jesus said that we must be born-again to enter the kingdom of Heaven. **Dead people** *don't go to heaven*, only *the **Live Ones** do—the spiritually alive*! Spiritually dead means separated from the life of God—without His Holy Spirit dwelling in us.

You were born a forgiven person—you just didn't know it, because of all the *out of context* teaching you've been taught over the years. You don't have to keep asking for what you already have, *forgiveness*! Jesus already paid for your sins, you just need to *believe* and *internalize it* in your *spirit*, the center of your being. Want more proof? (Heb. 10:16-17), "This is the *covenant* that I will make with them, after those days(after the death of Jesus) says the Lord: I will put My laws upon their heart, and on their mind I will write them, and their **sins** and **lawless** deeds **I will remember no more**." How's that for proof? After the crucifixion, the

Word of God says that He no longer remembers our sin. Wow, what a mind-blowing concept, huh? It takes a little faith, yet when you're finally able to internalize this truth, you won't *feel guilty* and *condemned* ever again! Only thankful and confident that you have finally found the truth and can now **rest** in God's forgiveness.

I recommend that you start reading and listening to New Covenant scriptures *daily*, and don't listen to *out of context* teaching in the brick buildings for at least 6 months. This will help you begin to unlearn (deprogram) your mind from all the years of *out of context* teachings you've been subjected to! Then faith will come to you as the Holy Spirit confirms to your spirit the truth concerning the *New Covenant*, and in the work that Jesus accomplished on the cross with regard to your sin. (Rom. 10:17) says, "*Faith comes* by **hearing**, and hearing by the Word of God." You must **hear** the Word of God in the *correct* context in order for faith to come. And don't just read it but read it ***out loud***, so that you can **hear** it, *then faith will come*. **Unbelief keeps asking** God to forgive you, while faith says **thank you** Father, that you don't remember my sin.

The apostle Paul said in (Eph. 5:20), "Always *giving thanks* for *all* things in the name of our Lord Jesus Christ."

What does *all things* mean? *Every word* in scripture is important, the word *all* means *ALL*! *All things* means that *even when we sin*, we can *give God thanks* that *He doesn't remember* our sin. That's walking by faith, not by sight. (2 Cor. 5:7) says, "for we walk by faith not by sight." Instead of focusing on our sin and feeling guilt and condemnation over it, we should ***focus on what Jesus did*** with regard to our sin. He ***took it away from before God's eyes*** by shedding His blood on the cross to pay for your past, present, and future sin. God has already provided forgiveness, you just need to receive it into your spirit by faith and learn to forgive yourself.

Under Mosaic Law(the Old Covenant), the Jewish sinner would have to bring an *animal sacrifice* to the priest in the temple, to *shed its blood* on the altar as a sin offering to receive forgiveness. However, under the New Covenant, Jesus is our High Priest and His ***blood has already been shed*** for the sin of the *world* (which includes you and me), by His death on the cross. (Col. 1:13-14) states, "His beloved Son, in whom ***we have redemption***, the *forgiveness of sins*." Not as most preachers say, that we have *to keep asking for it*, but that *we **have** it*—the forgiveness of sins!

When you've realized that you have broken one of God's laws, I've found this to be a faithful prayer to God for the New Covenant believer; 'Father, I'm sorry I did that, I didn't trust you enough Lord, help me to trust you more Lord, and **thank you** Father that You **don't remember** my sin.' This is a prayer of *true faith* in the finished work of our Lord and Savior Jesus Christ. Remember the last words Jesus said before He bowed His head and gave up His spirit, "**It is finished**" (John 19:30). (Rom. 6:23) says, "*The wages of sin is death.*" The *wages* for the world's sin had been paid, **Jesus died**!

When Jesus came to John to be baptized, after Jesus came up out of the water in (John 1:32-33) John testified saying,

> "I have seen the Spirit (Holy Spirit) *descending* as a dove out of heaven, and He (the Holy Spirit) remained on Him(Jesus)." I did not recognize Him, but He who sent me to baptize in water said to me, "He upon whom you see the Spirit *descending* and *remaining* on Him, this is the One who *baptizes in the Holy Spirit*."

Notice that the Holy Spirit came down from heaven and remained upon Him, because He was sinless. The only sin attributable to man *after the crucifixion* is **unbelief**. Jesus paid for all other sins. Once you repent of your unbelief you become sinless in God's eyes, and the Holy Spirit will *descend* and **remain in you**, clothing you in His(Jesus's) righteousness. (Heb.13:5) states, "I will never desert you, nor will I ever forsake you." The Holy Spirit will never leave you even when you stumble(sin by breaking one of Gods laws or commandments). Once you come to faith in Lord Jesus(Yeshua), you have *Eternal Life* and have become a child of God. No longer will Satan be your father. The Holy Spirit will *never leave you* because of sin, because God doesn't remember your sin thanks to the work of Jesus on the cross. Allowing you to keep the *free gift of eternal life **forever**!*

Sin has been taken out of the equation by Jesus, as far as **salvation** is concerned. However, everyone is this world is under a type of law that can be described as the **law of consequences**. Common sense will tell you that if you do bad things, you will suffer bad consequences. And if you do good things, you will experience good consequences. However, neither has any bearing on your salvation. Think about it, if the Holy Spirit left you because of sin, no one would be saved. It would have to be called **temporary life** not **eternal life**! God's word clearly teaches that we have eternal life, and *eternal means forever*! Here is a verse of scripture that supports what I have just said, (Rom. 8:9-10) says, "However you are not in the flesh but **in the Spirit**, if indeed the Spirit of God dwells in you. But if anyone does not have the Spirit of Christ, *he does not belong to Him*. If Christ is in you, **though the body is dead because of sin**, yet the **spirit is alive** because of righteousness." It's saying that even though we sin at times, called (dead works), our body is dead to God but **our spirit is alive** because the Holy Spirit has clothed us in the righteousness of Christ! The law of sin and death has no power over us because we are new creations in Christ, the ecclesia, the born-again!

In (1 Cor. 3:16) the apostle Paul asked this question, "Do you not know that *you are a temple of God* and that the **Spirit** of God **dwells in you**?" In (Gal. 3:2) Paul asked another interesting question, "This is the only thing I want to find out from you: did you receive the **Spirit** by the *works of the Law*, or by *hearing with faith*? The apostle Paul was a master at getting to the point, he did not beat around the bush. He plainly said, you cannot receive the Holy Spirit by striving to keep the Law, you can only receive the Spirit by *hearing* about the New Covenant in Messiah Jesus and receiving it by faith! In (Gal. 3:23) he said, "Before *faith* came, we were kept in custody *under the Law*, being shut up to the faith which was later to be revealed. Therefore the *Law has become our **tutor*** to *lead us* to Christ, so that we may be justified by faith. But *now that faith has come*, we are ***no longer under a tutor*.**" The purpose of the Law is to lead us to Christ, by showing us we are sinners in need of a savior. After the cross, we are no longer to be led by the Law, we are to be led by the Holy Spirit who dwells in us! (Rom. 8:14) says "For all who are being *led by the Spirit* of God, *these are the* **sons of God**."

In (Acts 17:24) we read, "The God who made the world and all things in it, since He is Lord of heaven and earth, **does not *dwell* in temples made with hands** (brick buildings)." In the Old Covenant, the presence of God (His Holy Spirit) dwelt in the Holy of Holies in the innermost part of the temple. Mankind was separated from His presence by a veil which surrounded the Holy of Holies and could only be entered into once a year by the high priest on the Day of Atonement. Scripture says that when Jesus died on the cross the veil was torn from top to bottom, and the Holy Spirit came out from the Holy of Holies and now lives in the hearts(spirits) of New Covenant believers, resurrecting our *dead spirits making us **alive** together with Him*, and sealing us until the day of redemption (the day Jesus returns). "And Jesus cried out again with a loud voice, and yielded up His spirit. And behold, the veil of the temple was torn in two from top to bottom." (Matt. 27:50-51)

(Rom. 5:10) states, "For if while we were enemies (lost) we **were reconciled** to God through the death of His son, much more **having been reconciled**, we shall be **SAVED BY HIS LIFE**." *Were reconciled* is *past tense,* and reconciled means brought into harmony (with regards to our sin). We're not saved by His death, *only forgiven*. We're saved by His Life (His Holy Spirit), which comes to dwell in us at the time we come to faith in Him. You see, unlike most preachers teach, *we don't have a sin problem* as far as salvation is concerned, Jesus took care of that problem for us on the cross. We have a **death problem**. We are all *spiritually dead* until the Holy Spirit comes to dwell in our body. To borrow from Bob George, the only thing a *dead man* needs is **Life**, and the only life available to us is through Christ Jesus and His Holy Spirit!

In (John 14:16-17) Jesus said, "I will ask the Father, and He will give you another Helper, that He may be with you ***forever***; that is the Spirit of Truth, whom the world cannot receive, because it does not see Him or know Him, but you know Him because He abides with you and ***will be in you***."

Abides means to remain; the Holy Spirit will remain in you even if you stumble(*sin*) because God doesn't remember our sin thanks to the work of Jesus on the cross. *Will be in you* means to live or dwell inside you. And forever means, well you know...

Under the Old Covenant, when King David realized that he had sinned by having Bathsheba's husband Uriah the Hittite murdered by sending him to the front line of the war. David felt the presence of the Holy Spirit begin to leave him. David prayed, "Lord do not take your Holy Spirit from me" (Ps. 51:11). Keep in mind this was under the Law in the Old Covenant, before Jesus had paid for the sin of the world. Because David had sinned the Holy Spirit was leaving him, a man after God's own heart. However, now under the New Covenant the Holy Spirit will ***never leave us because of sin***, thanks to the work of our wonderful Savior Lord Jesus. Give Him praise for He is worthy!

(Heb. 7:25) says, "Therefore ***He*** is able also to ***save forever*** those who draw near to God through Him, since He always lives to make intercession for them." How can sin cause you to lose your salvation when New Covenant scripture clearly states that He is able to ***save you forever*** and that God doesn't remember our sin? I heard one preacher say that sin can cause you to fall out of fellowship with God. This New Covenant scripture totally ***exposes*** another false teaching of falling in and out of fellowship with God. You're either in fellowship (***saved***), or out of fellowship (***lost***). I've already shown you scriptures that say God *doesn't remember our sin*, and that He is *not counting our sins against us*, (these concepts are *true* in the Bible *only after the crucifixion* in the New Covenant). The punishment for sin is death— not being out of fellowship! Maybe this preacher should start reading more ***New Covenant*** scripture and less *obsolete* Old Covenant scripture. Then maybe he could start teaching ***truth in the correct context***!

God disciplines those He loves, and the Holy Spirit will not let you walk away from your Heavenly Father.

You are now a child of the living God with His Holy Spirit dwelling in you. How can you walk away from something that *dwells inside* you? The Holy Spirit will never leave you nor forsake you. He will always lead and guide you back to the path God has purposed for you. Don't listen to these *slick double-talking* Old Covenant preachers anymore if you want to find and keep the peace that surpasses all understanding! Find a preacher who teaches the New Covenant, and good luck, because they are few and far between. Now that Jesus has paid in full the price for our sin, the *Holy Spirit can remain* in us *forever*, because God is not counting our sins against us. He's not counting, *one* sin, *two* sins, *three* sins. I don't know about you, but that's the best news I've ever heard in my life, that God has forgiven me of *all* my sins, past, present, and future. Hallelujah, thank you Lord Jesus, you are my King! I am a forgiven person, I don't have to keep asking for what I already have, I just need to receive it by faith and *believe*.

Most, if not all religions, teach that by doing *more good works* than *bad works*, or by continually asking God to be *merciful* and to *forgive you* for your sin, it will guarantee your entry into heaven. However, in the New Covenant of Jesus Christ we're taught that salvation is *not a result of good works*, and that *being forgiven is not what saves you*, forgiveness only *prepares the way* for you to be saved. Christianity is not a religion. It is the **one true faith** in the **one true God**. Forgiveness has already been provided, but agnostics, atheists and other religions choose not to believe it. Either they refuse to believe that *Jesus is the Son of God*, that He shed His blood on the cross to pay for their sins or that He was raised from the dead. "And according to the Law, one may almost say, all things are cleansed with blood, and **without shedding of blood there is no forgiveness**" (Heb. 9:22).

The *only sin* attributable to man *after the cross* is *unbelief*, all other sins were taken away from before God's eyes at the cross, never to be remembered again. If you don't believe in Jesus, you can't receive the Holy Spirit (*be born-again*), and you will remain in *eternal spiritual death*. Yes, **you can be forgiven** and still **go to Hell**! Remember we're not saved by His death (only forgiven), we're saved by His Life(the Holy Spirit). We only need to *repent of our unbelief* to receive the Holy Spirit. Salvation is achieved only when the Holy Spirit comes to dwell inside your body (*the new temple*), which is called being born-again, and it is only possible through saving faith in the Lord Jesus Christ. Do you have ***saving faith*** in Lord Jesus? Do you believe ***on Him*** as your Lord and Savior and not just ***in Him*** as an historical figure? "For whosoever shall ***call upon the name*** of the Lord shall be saved" (Rom. 10:13).

CHAPTER 3

GRACE VS LAW

I n this chapter I will be emphasizing the difference between God's Old Covenant of Law and His New Covenant of grace. There are many examples of this difference, which are not being taught by most preachers. As I mentioned before in Chapter one, the beginning of understanding this concept of how to differentiate between Law and grace in God's word is found in Hebrews 9:16-17. Basically, ***any* teaching** in the Bible *before the crucifixion* of Christ, which *contradicts* what is taught *after the crucifixion* should be ***rejected*** as Old Covenant. The Law is for the lost, and the purpose of the Law is to lead the lost to Christ. The lost are under the condemnation of the Law, while we who are New Covenant believers are *not* under the condemnation of the Law. We have been enlightened to the fact that we are totally incapable of keeping the **_whole Law_**, and so we do not participate in biblical ignorance by beating ourselves up over our inability to do so. We turn to God for His grace, His favor that we don't deserve, through faith in what His Son did on our behalf, on the cross of Calvary. He *forgave us* and *we believe it*—it's called **_faith_**. The Holy Spirit sets us free from the law of sin and death. We are no longer lost under the Old Covenant of law which *judges and condemns* us to spiritual death because of our sin. We don't have to fear God's wrath or the Judgement Day or even death, because **_we're going to heaven when we die and we know it_**!

The reason most people keep asking God to forgive them is because they haven't fully embraced or don't understand what Jesus accomplished for them on the cross, and they *fear they will be judged* for their sins on Judgement Day. They don't realize there are literally hundreds of Laws/commandments they are not keeping. We can't **_cherry pick_** a few of God's commandments to keep some of the time in order to soothe our conscience, and think that puts us in right-standing with Him. Those who think like this are called *legalists* and are biblically ignorant of what the whole Law is, and about the wonderful grace God offers through His New Covenant in Christ Jesus. They are trying to *work and earn* their way into heaven, by **striving** to keep some of the commandments, some of the time. And when they fall short they ask God to forgive them, not realizing or believing that God forgave the *whole world* at the cross as it says in His word. Either way, spiritually it's not a good place to find yourself in, not sure if you're forgiven and not sure if you're saved, but they still **keep asking** for forgiveness just to be on the safe side! Not realizing that they are far, far away from the place of **rest** the Bible calls the "peace that surpasses all understanding."

Legalists are blissfully ignorant of the fact that there are a total of 613 laws and commandments in the Old Testament alone. These include 365 positive commandments (meaning to do certain things), and 248 negative commandments (meaning not to do certain things). And let us not forget the other 1,050 new commandments which Jesus gave us in the New Testament which we don't keep all the time. For example, Here are two commandments of Jesus found in (1 Cor. 13:4), "Love is patient, love is kind." Let's be honest now, are we always patient? Are we always kind? Just like me, you will have to say no I'm not always patient or always kind to others. You see, we can't even keep the love commandments.

I believe this is the very same argument the Apostle Paul had in the beginning of the early church with the religious leaders and even some of the Apostles. Paul was trying to explain New Covenant grace to them while they were arguing with him saying, what then, shall we just forget about the Law of Moses? This is the same thing the Jewish leaders accused Jesus of doing, saying He was violating the law of Moses. They called it *blasphemy*, and that is why they hated him and wanted to kill him. I've encountered this same **self-righteous religious spirit rearing its ugly head** in todays modern-day legalists, causing outrage in these so-called law keepers when I try to teach them about New Covenant grace. They're typical response is something like, "so I can just go out and rob a bank and kill 50 people, and I will still go to heaven?" People who ask outrageous questions like this are still trying to live under the Old Covenant of Law, and lack understanding and revelation knowledge about the New Covenant of grace. Maybe they've never heard what the Apostle Paul said in (Rom. 6:1),

"What shall we say then? Are we to continue in sin so that grace may increase? May it never be! How shall we who *died to sin* still live in it?" And (Rom. 5:20) where He said, "The law came in so that the transgression would increase; but where sin increased, grace abounded all the more." And don't forget, "**All things are lawful**, but not all things are profitable" in (1 Cor. 10:23).

Once we enter into this New Covenant with God through the blood of Jesus, nothing can separate us from the love of God, not even sin. Jesus paid for the world's sin, and the Word of God says He is no longer counting our sins against us. Once you *internalize this reality*, you will want to sin less and less, not more and more. You will no longer fear a Holy and righteous God and His Judgement Day. "There is *no fear* in love, because fear involves punishment, and the one who fears is not perfected in love" (1 John 4:18). His kindness *leads us* to repentance, and we love Him because He first loved us. (Gal. 5:13-14) says, "For you were called to freedom, brethren; only do not turn your freedom into an opportunity for the flesh, but through love serve one another. For the whole law is fulfilled in one word, in the statement, "**You shall love your neighbor as yourself**" (Gal. 5:14). After you come to understand the perfect love of

God, and how He has **already forgiven you** of **all** your sin, past, present, and future sin, then you will find it much easier *to _forgive_* those who've sinned against you.

God's Law reveals our sin in the same way a mirror reveals the dirt on our face. The Law can never remove our sin, it can only reveal it, just as a mirror cannot remove the dirt from your face. The Old Covenant of Law *revealed the sin* of mankind, while the New Covenant of Grace *removed the sin* of mankind. The blood of Jesus washed away our sin. I understand the legalists predicament because at one time I too was a legalist, caught in the *vicious cycle* of feeling guilt and condemnation, knowing that I was not always keeping God's commandments. I was continually having to ask God to forgive me for my sins, over and over again. Especially after finding out about what God's word said, that "man looks at the outward appearance but the **Lord looks at the heart**" (1 Sam. 16:7). That prompted me to look deeper into my own heart, realizing that nothing is hidden from the Lord and that I could not faithfully keep even the first Ten commandments, in my flesh or in my heart—at all times. I finally came to the understanding that God's Law is perfect but that I was not! Jesus was God in the flesh, while I am only flesh with His Holy Spirit living in me. And that's why He could keep *all the laws—all the time,* He's God and I'm not. The law brought me to my knees, to the ***end of myself*** trying to make myself righteous before a Holy God through my own works of trying to keep His Law. Apart from Jesus we have no righteousness, and the only righteousness we do have is through His Holy Spirit *dwelling* in us, **clothing us in His righteousness**.

Just as it says, "Therefore the Law has become our tutor to *lead us* to Christ" (Gal. 3:24). The purpose of the law is to *lead us* to Christ. The Law showed me that I am a sinner and that I cannot earn or work my way into God's heaven by trying to keep the Law. I am an utter failure when it comes to trying to keep God's 1663 laws and commandments at all times. If you're honest with God you will come to the same conclusion. You will never be more holy than what Jesus has already made you by sending His Holy Spirit to live inside you! Under the Old Covenant **before the cross,** the Israelites would try to keep the Law to be righteous, then once a year bring a sin offering to the temple to get forgiven for their sins. But under the New Covenant ***Jesus is our sin offering***, and the apostle Paul said in (Rom. 10:4), "For Christ is the ***end of the Law for righteousness*** to everyone *who believes*." The Holy Spirit dwelling inside you is now what makes you perfectly righteous! Do you believe?

CHAPTER 4

JESUS IS OUR
SABBATH REST

J esus said, "Come to Me all who are weary and heavy laden, and I will give you _rest_. For My yoke is easy and My burden is light" (Matt. 11:28,30). Once the Holy Spirit reveals the *truth* about the New Covenant to you, the *REAL* good news of the Gospel of Jesus Christ. And after the Law has completed its purpose by bringing you to *end of yourself* of striving to keep it. When you finally surrender your self-righteousness for **_His true righteousness_**, by coming to the realization that you cannot keep *all the laws—all the time*, only then will you be able to embrace the *'rest'* that Jesus offers you. "He made Him who knew no sin to be sin on our behalf, so that we might become the righteousness of God in Him" (2 Cor. 5:21).

Once you understand the love and grace God offers you as His child, you will find the "peace that surpasses all comprehension." It can only be found when you *cease from your works* and learn to *rest in His finished work*. "For the one who has **entered HIS rest** has himself also **rested from his works**" (Heb. 4:10). As long as we are trying to enter in by faith in *our works*, we will never be able to enter *His rest*. Because of our disobedience—our lack of faith in Jesus and *His* work, we will continue to remain in a type of **spiritual wilderness**. Not confident about our salvation, always striving to keep the Law feeling condemned in our inability to do so, and never being able to enter **His rest** (*our promised land*), in understanding the ***finality of the cross***! "When you were dead in your transgressions and the uncircumcision of your flesh, He made you alive together with Him, ***having forgiven us all our transgressions***, having canceled out the certificate of debt consisting of decrees against us, which was hostile to us; and He has taken it out of the way, having nailed it to the cross" (Col. 2:13-14).

(Heb. 4:6,9,10,11) states, "So there remains a **Sabbath rest** for the people of God. Therefore, since is remains for some to enter it, and those who formerly had good news preached to them failed to enter because of disobedience, for the one who has entered **His rest**, has himself also rested from **his works**, as God did from His. Therefore, let us be *diligent* to enter that rest, so that no one will fall, through following the same example of disobedience." Jesus said, "Come to me and I will give you rest." Have **you** entered His New Covenant rest?

After creation was completed, scripture says that God **rested** on the seventh day, and that is why Old Covenant Jewish believers go to the temple, and do no work on the *Sabbath Day* or seventh day of the week. This was one of the Ten Commandments which stated, "Remember the Sabbath Day to keep it holy. Six days you shall labor and do all your work, but the seventh day is a sabbath of the Lord your God; in it you shall not do any work, you or your son or your daughter, your male or your female servant or your cattle or your sojourner who stays with you" (Exod. 20:8-10). However, we as New

Covenant believers have a new commandment concerning the Sabbath day, found in (Col. 2:16-17), which **supercedes** the Old Covenant commandment about keeping the Sabbath Day holy. It states, "Therefore **no one is to act as your judge** in regard to **food** or **drink** or in respect to a festival or a new moon or a **Sabbath day**— things which are a *mere shadow* of what is to come; but the substance belongs to Christ." The Law was a *shadow* of Christ, who was to come and who now has come! As New Covenant believers we don't rest or worship God on one certain day of the week. We *rest* in His finished work, and worship Christ **in our hearts everyday** of the week! While orthodox Jewish believers still go to temple on Saturday, we Christians gather together on Sunday, to commemorate the *resurrection* of Jesus on the first day of the week. We have a New Covenant commandment which states "not forsaking our own assembling together, as is the habit of some, but encouraging one another; and all the more as you see the day drawing near" (Heb. 10:25).

The New Covenant teaches us believers that our bodies have become the *new temple* of the Holy Spirit, so we can now praise and worship God in our hearts *anytime* and *anywhere*! (Acts 17:24) says, "God does not dwell in temples made with hands." (Rom. 12:1) says, "to present your bodies a *__living__* and *__holy__* sacrifice, acceptable to God, which is your *spiritual* service of *__worship__*"!

CHAPTER 5

FORGIVEN OR NOT FORGIVEN

During the brief period of Jesus's ministry, about three years, He was **under the Old Covenant** of Law, which is recorded in the four gospels of Matthew, Mark, Luke, and John. Remember, the New Covenant did not **go into force** until Jesus died. It's my opinion that since Jesus lived under the Old Covenant of Law, that the four gospels should have been placed at the end of the Old Testament after Malachi, not at the beginning of the New Testament! This I believe, would have stopped most of this confusion about where to *rightly divide* the word of truth. It's also important to recognize that at the end of *each of the four gospels,* an account is given of the death, burial, and resurrection. The point I am trying to make is that after the first account of the crucifixion and resurrection at the end of the book of Matthew. You could actually *skip over* Mark, Luke, and John to the Book of Acts, and you would then be in the New Covenant section of the Bible! But the way things are, right after the crucifixion and resurrection at the end of the book of Matthew, the very next chapter begins with the book of Mark, and that puts you right back under the context of the Old Covenant of Law again. I'm talking about *context*. You can see the confusion this might cause if you don't recognize the correct context of the four gospels. Now maybe you can see why I said that in my opinion, the four gospels should have been placed *at the end* of the Old Testament, and *not at the beginning* of the New Testament. Because ninety-nine percent of *all four gospels* are *under the Old Covenant of Law* right up to the different accounts of the crucifixion!

With this in mind maybe now you can understand why I say that some of the teachings which Lord Jesus taught while living under the Old Covenant of Law do not apply to us today, because we are under His New Covenant of Grace. Most of the teachings of Lord Jesus *do apply* to us, but not the ones that *contradict* what is said *after the cross* in the New Covenant, which begins with the Book of Acts. One example of a contradiction is found in the Lord's Prayer, in the Book of Matthew. Most preachers teach that the Lord's Prayer is a proper way for believers to pray today. They are *totally wrong*! First of all, the proper context is that He was talking to Jews living under the Old Covenant of Law when He gave this teaching on prayer! In (Matt. 6:12) Jesus said, "Forgive us our debts, as we also have forgiven our debtors." Here Jesus is telling His disciples to **ask God to forgive them** for their sins. This prayer was given under the Old Covenant of Law (before Jesus died), and was a proper prayer for anyone under the Old Covenant. However, under the New Covenant of Grace, we've learned that our sins **have already been forgiven** at the cross and that we are **forgiven persons**. And that under this New Covenant of Grace, we don't have to keep asking for what we already have; **forgiveness**!

(Heb. 10:8-12,14) states, "Sacrifices and offerings and whole burnt offerings and sacrifices for sin You have not desired, nor have You taken pleasure in them" (which are offered according to the Law), He takes away the first (covenant) in order to establish the second (covenant). By this will we *have been sanctified* through the offering of the body of Jesus Christ ***once for all***. Every priest stands daily ministering and offering time after time the same sacrifices, which can ***never take away sins***; but He, having offered ***one sacrifice*** for sins ***for all time***, sat down at the right hand of God. For by one offering He has ***perfected for all time*** those who are sanctified."

Sanctified means to be *set apart* and *made holy* (by faith in His sacrifice). Notice here that it says, Jesus has *perfected for all time* those who come to Him by faith. Could this be what He was alluding to when He was under Law and said in (Matt. 5:48), "Therefore you are to be *perfect*, as your Heavenly Father is perfect." Most believers commonly mistake this teaching as meaning that you have to be perfect in your flesh in obedience to the Law,(good luck with that)! Since we can't become perfect in our flesh in this fallen world, it's Jesus who makes us perfect, ***perfectly righteous in our spirit*** (in right standing with God) when His Holy Spirit comes to *live in us*. And let me not forget to mention, it also said He offered ***one sacrifice*** for ***sins*** for ***all time***! How's that for *good news*? Hallelujah thank you Jesus!

(Heb.10:15,16,17) then says, And the Holy Spirit also testifies to us; for after saying,

> "This is the Covenant that I will make with them *After those days*, says the Lord: I will put My ***laws*** upon their heart, And on their mind I will write them, " He then says, "And their ***sins*** and their ***lawless*** deeds. I will ***REMEMBER NO MORE***."

Notice He didn't say, I will put **My Law** upon their heart, He said **My laws**(small l). The apostle Paul spoke of this saying, "Where then is boasting? It is excluded. By what kind of law? Of works? No, but by a ***law of faith***.

For we maintain that a man is **justified by faith** *apart from works* of the Law" (Rom. 3:27).

We have been browbeaten in the brick buildings for years to have faith in the scriptures given under the *Old Covenant* of Law. But I am encouraging you now my brothers and sisters in Christ, to have faith in God's word which begins with the Book of Acts after the crucifixion, under the *New Covenant* of Grace. We are **forgiven persons** *after* the cross. We don't have to keep asking for it, *we have* **forgiveness of sins**. As I said before, once you understand the correct context of God's word, it all makes perfect sense. And you will find this is the *only way* that it makes sense. Hebrews 8:13, teaches that the Old Covenant system of offering animal sacrifices for the forgiveness of sin is now **obsolete**. "Now where there is forgiveness of these things, **there is no longer any offering for sin**" (Heb. 10:18). Are you going to continue trying to live under an *obsolete* Old Covenant which is no longer valid (under condemnation of the Law), or are you going to *walk by faith* in the finished work of Jesus, under the New Covenant of Grace (in forgiveness and freedom) which God has already provided for you? God will not accept any other offering for sin other than the one He *has already offered* for you, through the death of His Son.

Do you now see why we are not walking by faith but by ***presumption*** and ***unbelief*** when we keep asking God to forgive us, when His word says that He has already *forgiven us at the cross*? Jesus is not going to get back up on the cross and shed His blood again every time you ask God to forgive you. When you're tempted to ask God for forgiveness again through force of habit, say these four Bible verses ***out loud***;

(John 3:18), "He who ***believes*** in Him is ***not judged***." (Heb. 9:22), "***Without shedding of blood*** *there is* ***no forgiveness***." (Heb.7:25), "He is able also to ***save forever*** those who draw near to God ***through Him***." And (2 Cor. 5:19), "God was in Christ reconciling the ***world*** to Himself, ***not counting their trespasses*** against them."

These four Bible verses will give you confidence and assurance that you are a forgiven person, and that you don't have to keep asking God for what you already have! God forgave the world's sin(which includes your sin and my sin) at the cross. This helps to explain what I said before about the Lord's Prayer being an Old Covenant obsolete prayer and does not apply to New Covenant believers today. We don't have to keep asking for forgiveness because God forgave the ***world*** at the cross. We just need to ***receive it*** and ***believe it***, and not just in our head *but in our heart*. I've heard many preachers teach that you have keep short accounts with God by asking Him to forgive you for your sins. And then the very next Sunday teach just the opposite, that Jesus paid for your sins by shedding His blood on the cross! This is ***double-talk***, and most intelligent people should be able to see the contradiction. No wonder so many believers are confused about forgiveness today.

I'm sure that by now some of you students of the Bible may have a question forming in the back of your mind concerning (1 John 1:9), am I right? If so, very good, that shows you're thinking. This is another widespread ***out of context*** teaching that needs to be exposed. It states, "If we confess our sins, He is faithful and righteous to forgive us our sins, and to cleanse us of all unrighteousness" (1 John 1:9). In the entire New Testament, it's the only time that the words forgiveness and confession are mentioned together in the same verse! That should be a red flag to any thinking Bible student of the New Covenant that the context warrants further investigation. First of all, the correct context here is that John is addressing the lost, not believers. Bob George had this to say about it;

In about 90 A.D., a heretical group, which was a forerunner of the Gnostics, was teaching that mankind was without sin. That all *matter* is evil and only *spirit* is good, and that Jesus couldn't have come in the flesh, because flesh is matter. They believed that Jesus was only an illusion.

Think about it, if Jesus hadn't come in the flesh He could not have been crucified to pay for our sins. By denying that Jesus had come in the flesh was to deny the Gospel. In (1 John 1:8), the verse just before (1 John 1:9) it says, "If we say that we have no sin, we are deceiving ourselves and **the truth is not in us**." If the **truth** is not in us, the Holy Spirit, the Spirit of Truth, was not in them, so they weren't believers, they were **unbelievers**! Bob George explained it like this;

It's as if John was saying to them, "I don't know if you are ever going to come to your senses, and <u>agree with God</u> concerning your sins. But, if at anytime — today, tomorrow or whenever you should decide to turn to Him, God can be depended upon to have forgiven your sins and to have cleansed you of all unrighteousness."

(1 John 1:9) is a **_salvation passage_**, not a teaching that you must ask God to forgive you every time you sin. That would totally contradict ninety-nine percent of the other teachings in the New Covenant! As I said before, even in the New Covenant it's important to understand the correct context of scripture to keep from being confused.

Most people come to faith in Jesus for salvation and to be forgiven for their sins. No follower of Christ in his right mind is going to say, I've never sinned. You have to agree with God that you are a sinner, in order to be saved! Also, _confessing your sin_ is different than _asking for forgiveness_. I highly recommend that you do **confess your sins** _to God_, each time the Holy Spirit convicts you, to purify your heart and to keep a clean conscience, continually drawing near to Him. But that's with the knowledge and understanding that you were already forgiven at the cross. "Let us **draw near** with a sincere heart in full assurance of faith, having our hearts sprinkled clean from an evil conscience and our bodies washed with pure water" (Heb. 10:22).

To confess to something is to _admit_ to doing it (admitting that you have sinned). If you were being interrogated by the police about your involvement in a crime and you confessed to it, you're **not asking for forgiveness** you're **admitting guilt**. I invite you to do some research for yourself as to the proper context of 1 John 1:9. You will find that many preachers have been teaching it out of context for many years and **most** continue to do so! Also be aware of the context change that happens when (1 John chapter 1) changes from **writing to Gnostics**, to (1 John chapter 2) where he is **writing to believers** where he says, "My little children, I am writing these things to you so that you may not sin. And if anyone sins, we have and Advocate with the Father, Jesus Christ the righteous; and He Himself is the propitiation(means to appease God) for our sins; and not for ours only, but also for those of the **whole world**" (1 John 2:1-2). There it is again, now John is saying that Jesus paid for the sins of not only believers, but **the whole world**.

The apostle Paul taught what we must do in order to be saved, "that if you confess with your mouth Jesus as Lord, and believe in your heart that God raised Him from the dead, **you will be saved**" (Rom. 10:9). Did you notice that Paul didn't mention anything about asking God for forgiveness as a prerequisite to being saved? That's because He knew that **forgiveness was a given**, and had already been accomplished at the cross. There is no longer any forgiveness to be executed on your behalf. (John 3:18-19) states, "He who believes in Him **is not judged**; he who does not believe has been *__judged already__*, because he has not believed in the name of the only begotten Son of God." Here, it's saying that if you believe in Jesus you will *not be judged*! This exposes another false teaching by many preachers who say that believers will be judged for their sins!

The reason most believers keep asking God to forgive them is because they haven't been taught the difference between the Old and New Covenants, and they believe that they are going to be judged for their sins on Judgement Day,(thanks again, preachers). Believers are not going to be judged for their sins, because Jesus already paid for the sins of the world? Jesus took our judgement on the cross, and we receive that forgiveness joyfully—**by faith**. Unbelievers are already judged they just haven't been sentenced yet! Believers are going to be *rewarded/recompensed* on Judgement Day for their **good works**. I will give you scriptural proof of this fact in a later chapter.

"Therefore let it be known to you, brethren, that through Him forgiveness of sins is proclaimed to you, and through Him ***everyone who believes is freed from ALL things***, from which you ***could not be freed through the Law*** of Moses" (Acts 13:38-39). Freed from ***all things*** includes being ***free from fear*** of being judged on ***Judgement Day*** for your sin. We can be confident Judgement Day for believers will be more like an ***Awards Ceremony***! He who knew no sin paid a debt He did not owe, for me a sinner who owed a debt I could not pay. Praise His holy name for He is worthy!

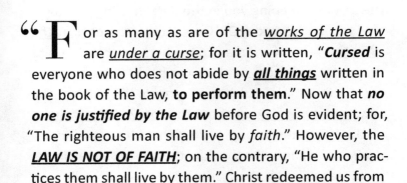

CHAPTER 6

THE LAW IS
NOT OF FAITH

❝ **F**or as many as are of the <u>works of the Law</u> are <u>under a curse</u>; for it is written, "**Cursed** is everyone who does not abide by **_all things_** written in the book of the Law, **to perform them**." Now that **no one is justified by the Law** before God is evident; for, "The righteous man shall live by *faith*." However, the **_LAW IS NOT OF FAITH_**; on the contrary, "He who practices them shall live by them." Christ redeemed us from the *curse of the Law*, having become a **curse** for us—for

73

it is written, "Cursed is everyone who hangs on a tree"—in order that in Christ Jesus the blessing of Abraham might come to the Gentiles, so that we would receive the ***promise of the Spirit*** through faith" (Gal. 3:10-14).

The curse of the Law is that we as human beings in the flesh cannot keep *all the laws—all the time* like Jesus did. He was God in human flesh, incapable of sinning. Did you catch what the apostle Paul said about the ***Law is not of faith***. Bet you never heard a preacher mention that verse of scripture before! ***Most preachers avoid it***, because it would expose all of the *out of context*, false teachings they've been spewing for the past thirty or forty years. Or maybe they don't want you to understand it so they can keep you from knowing the truth by keeping you in the dark, making you think that you are still under Old Covenant Law, especially ***the tithe Law***! I've heard many preachers teach right up to that verse and stop, or skip over it and go to the next verse about Christ redeeming us from the curse of the Law, *not saying a word* about the ***Law is not of faith***.

Don't get me wrong, it's not that I have a vendetta against preachers. I'm thankful that we have men in the pulpit teaching us about Jesus. However, it really rubs me the wrong way me when I hear some preacher trying to mix Law and Grace, causing confusion and deceiving the sheep! He's probably causing more harm than good. If a preacher doesn't know the difference between the Old and New Covenants he should get out of the pulpit, and let someone else who does know, do the preaching!

CHAPTER 7

FIRST FRUITS
OR TITHING

A s I mentioned before, there are many differences between the New and Old Covenants, here is yet another example of that difference. Under the Old Covenant there was a law called the tithe. The tithe law was given to the nation of Israel under the Old Covenant of Law. (Mal.3:8-9) says, "Will a man rob God? Yet you are robbing Me! But you say, 'How have we robbed You?' In tithes and offerings. You are cursed with a curse, for you are robbing Me, the **_whole nation_** of you!" What

Nation was God talking about? The **_nation of Israel_**, there were no Christians at the time the book of Malachi was written! Yet most modern-day preachers teach that we Christians are under the Old Covenant tithe law! This is another false and out of context teaching preachers like to beat us over the head with. The book of Malachi was written approximately 400 years **_before_** the birth of Jesus! As I said many times, it's very important to understand the context of scripture. The book of Malachi is located in the Old Testament under the Old Covenant of Law. We are under the New Covenant of Grace which was ushered in after Jesus died on the cross.

The original way of giving an offering to God was called FIRST FRUITS. It was first mentioned in the book of Genesis hundreds of years before the Law was given to Moses, beginning with the story of Cain and Abel his brother. In (Gen. 4:4-5) we find, "Abel, on his part brought an offering to the Lord of the **_firstlings_** of his flock, which pleased God, and the Lord had regard for Abel and his offering; but for Cain and for his offering He had no regard. Cain became very angry and his countenance fell." Cain brought an offering to the Lord of the fruit of the ground, but it was not the **first fruits**. God told Cain "If *you do well*, (referring to **giving the**

first part of the harvest) will not your countenance be lifted up? And if you do not do well, **sin is crouching** at the door; and its desire is for you, but **you must master it**" (Gen. 4:7). So here, God is saying that to do well, you must honor Him and His kingdom by giving the **first fruits** of ALL your increase, whatever it may be (harvest, flock, or income). And that if you do not do well, (**by not giving the first part** of all your increase), sin will have its desire and will be master over you. I believe that the act of giving our first fruits to God is an important biblical principle, one of the keys needed to unlock or unblock the (**blessings pipeline**)! "Honor the Lord from your wealth and from the **first** of **all** your produce; So your barns will be filled with plenty and your vats will overflow with new wine" (Proverbs 3:9-10). Remember God looks at the heart, and giving Him the *first part* of **All** your increase shows that you are putting Him first, even in your finances. Giving God the first part of all your increase will definitely lift your countenance and increase your faith! It's *remarkable* how it gives you a sense of well-being. You will begin to see prayers being answered and mountains will start to move when you put God first in your finances! It takes faith to do it, and that's the reason He honors it. Remember, without faith it is impossible to please Him!

Now, let's fast forward to the New Covenant teaching about giving. The apostle Paul said, "Each one must do(or give) just as he has purposed in his heart, not grudgingly or under compulsion, for God loves a cheerful giver" (2 Cor. 9:7). In the New Covenant, we are not under compulsion(being forced) to give a certain percentage of our income to avoid being cursed with a curse, as they were under Old Covenant tithe law. Abraham gave Melchizedek a **tenth** of (the choicest) of all the spoils, as he was returning from the slaughter of the kings—and Melchizedek **blessed** him. This was mentioned in the Old Testament in (Gen. 14:20) before the Law was given, and again in the New Covenant in (Heb. 7:2) by the apostle Paul.

Jesus taught us to give to the poor, orphans, and widows, and that by doing so we would be storing up treasure in heaven. "For where your treasure is, there your heart will be also" (Luke 12:34). The apostle Paul said to give to anyone who *ministers truth* to you. If someone is teaching that you are under Old Covenant tithe law, they are not ministering truth! God doesn't need gold and silver or fruits and vegetables! It all belongs to Him anyway. The real purpose for bringing the tithe into the storehouse under the Old Covenant, was for the support of the levitical priesthood. The Bible clearly states that the whole nation of Israel was *cursed with a curse* for not bringing "the whole tithe into the storehouse, so that there may be **_food_** in My house" (Mal. 9-10). This food was to be used to support the priests and their families. Priests were not allowed to have a job or to own property, so this was their only means of support. The burnt offerings were to be used for their meat(barbecue—yummy), and the produce was their fruit and vegetables, not to mention the oil, wine and flour. The gold, silver, and whatever else was taken in was also to be used for the support of the priests and their families. Read Numbers chapter 18 beginning at verse 8 called "The Priests' Portion."

Todays preachers are not under such restrictions. They are allowed to own property and to have other incomes such as a job, or even their own business. Instead of trusting God to supply the needs of their ministry, most preachers these days are teaching that **_you_** are cursed with a curse if you don't give them ten-percent of your income. Trying to put us New Covenant believers back under Old Covenant tithe law! Now they've turned their brick and mortar buildings into a **den of thieves**, worse than the money changers in the temple back in Jesus's day. Turning it into a money-making business instead of feeding the sheep the truth about the New Covenant. And they've been getting away with it for decades. That's why you see so many multi-millionaire preachers these days especially on television, bringing their false teaching about the tithe law to millions of viewers around the world. To many who barely have enough extra money to pay their utility bill. While the preacher is living in a multi-million dollar house, driving around in Cadillac's and Rolls Royces, wearing Rolex watches and flying on their private jets! I won't mention any names, but I had one friend who attended one of the (brick buildings) in Atlanta Georgia regularly. He told me the pastor was demanding that everyone attending his (church) had to bring him a copy of their income tax return. He wanted to make sure he was getting his ten percent!

That's the root cause of most of our countries problems now. Most preachers have become ***lovers of money*** more than lovers of God, and have bowed the knee to the government to get tax exempt status through their 501(c)(3) organization. A law called the Johnson

Amendment, adopted in 1954, prohibits preachers from speaking out about any political campaign on behalf or in opposition to anyone running for public office. We need preachers with a back-bone who will stand up to the government and tell the truth about the politicians who are running for office instead of kowtowing to the government to get more money! That's why we have so many immoral politicians in office now making laws that are contrary to the Word of God and destroying the very foundation of our government. One of our founding fathers John Adams, said that our Constitution was made for a ***moral*** and ***religious*** People. And that it is wholly inadequate to the government of any other!

"Christ redeemed us from the curse of the Law, having become a curse for us—for it is written, "Cursed is everyone who hangs on a tree" (Gal. 3:13). This verse of scripture states that New Covenant believers are <u>not under a curse</u> for not keeping the Law, and as it pertains to this chapter, this includes the tithe law. Jesus removed the curse from us by becoming a curse for us. The apostle Paul said, "He who sows (or gives) sparingly shall also reap sparingly, and he who sows bountifully shall also reap bountifully" (2 Cor. 9:6). These are New Covenant principles of giving, not the Old Covenant Law of tithing. Under Old Covenant Law the punishment for sin was death. Paul said, that as many as are under the Law are under a curse if they do not abide by **all things** written in the Book of the Law, to perform them. The power of sin is in the Law. The curse of the Law is death, spiritual death and even physical death in some cases under the Old Covenant. However, under the New Covenant the Bible says that the Holy Spirit lives in us, giving us **eternal life**, which sets us free from the curse of the Law of sin and death! New Covenant believers are not under a curse for not keeping the *tithe Law*!

Here's another difference between Old Covenant tithe Law and the New Covenant of Grace that I find very interesting. In the Old Covenant it said that if the Israelites paid the *tithe*, that **God** "would open for you the windows of heaven and pour out for you a blessing until it overflows" (Mal. 3:10). Compare that to what Jesus said in (Luke 6:38), "Give and it will be given to you. **They** (men) will pour into your lap a good measure—pressed down, shaken together, and running over. Under the Old Covenant it said that **God would pour out for you** a blessing, while under the New Covenant Jesus said that **they/men would pour into your lap**. Interesting comparison wouldn't you say?

Jesus gave very clear instruction about who we should give to. He said to give to the ***poor,*** to ***orphans,*** and to ***widows*** in order to store up treasure in heaven. However, if you want to start receiving blessings while here on earth, do as God says in (Gen. 12:3), "And I will bless those who bless you." He was speaking of the ***nation of Israel***. Begin giving your *first-fruits* to the kingdom of God by giving to charities supporting Israel and you will prosper and be blessed here and now in this world! As I said before if someone is teaching you that you are under Old Covenant tithe law, they are ***not ministering truth***. Paul said to grow in the ***grace of giving*** not the ***law of tithing***! "But seek *first* His kingdom and His righteousness, and all these things will be added to you" (Matt. 6:33). "Honor the Lord from your wealth, And from the ***first*** of ***all*** your produce; So your barns will be filled with plenty, And your vats will overflow with new wine" (Proverbs 3:9-10)!

CHAPTER 8

THE
UNFORGIVABLE SIN

W hat is blasphemy? A question I've been asked many times. Blasphemy has been called the unforgivable sin, and so it is, especially if it is directed against the Holy Spirit. I will give some examples to help you understand its meaning. But for now, the short answer is that it's basically **_unbelief_**.

The only unforgivable sin I have found in the Bible is the sin of unbelief. All other sins were forgiven at the time of the crucifixion of Jesus, past, present, and future sins. Here are a couple of examples of unbelief which are mentioned in the scriptures;

> After Jesus had chosen the twelve Apostles, sending them out to preach and giving them authority to cast out demons. "The scribes who came down from Jerusalem were saying, "He is possessed by Beelzebul, " and "He cast out the demons by the ruler of the demons" (Mark 3:22). In other words, they were saying that the power (the Holy Spirit) Jesus used to cast out demons, was an evil or unclean spirit. Jesus answered them and said; "Truly I say to you, ***all sins shall be forgiven*** the sons of men, and whatever blasphemies they utter; but whoever blasphemes against the Holy Spirit never has forgiveness, but is guilty of an eternal sin." If you call the Holy Spirit evil or unclean, how can you be saved?

They ***didn't believe*** it was the Holy Spirit of God that gave Jesus His power because they were saying, "He has an unclean spirit" (Mark 3:30).

Another example of unbelief and its consequences can be found in (Heb. 10:26-29) where it states, "For if we go on sinning willfully (continue in unbelief) after receiving the knowledge of the truth, there no longer remains a sacrifice for sins, but a terrifying expectation of judgement and the ***fury of a fire*** which will consume the adversaries. Anyone who has set aside the Law of Moses *dies without mercy* on the testimony of two or three witnesses. How much severer punishment do you think he will deserve who has trampled underfoot the Son of God, and has regarded as unclean the blood of the Covenant by which he was sanctified, and has insulted the ***Spirit of Grace***? The definition of blasphemy is the act of offense of speaking sacrilegiously about God or sacred things. It appears that ***unbelief*** encompasses both of these acts or offenses of calling the Holy Spirit unclean, or ***not believing*** that the shed blood of Lord Jesus was the final sacrifice for sin, and that God will not accept any other offering for sin. (Heb. 10:18) states, "Now where there is forgiveness for these things, there is no longer any offering for sin." That's why I said before, that to keep asking God to forgive you is ***not walking by faith***, but is actually an act of ***unbelief***! Be very careful to make sure that you have ***saving faith***!

CHAPTER 9

DIETARY LAWS VS DIETARY GRACE

The Apostle Paul said in the New Covenant, "One person has faith that he may eat **_all things_**, but he who is weak (weak in faith), eats vegetables only" (Rom. 14:2). Some religions forbid the eating of certain meats. The Old Covenant Jewish religion is no exception. In Leviticus chapter 11 in the Old Testament, you can find the description of certain insects, birds, animals and fish that are either allowed or forbidden to eat, under the Old Covenant of Law. The following example is a partial list of creatures that are deemed ***unclean*** according to Old Covenant scripture; the camel, shaphan, rabbit, pig, eagle, buzzard, kite, falcon, raven, owl, seagull, ostrich, hawk, pelican, carrion vulture, stork, heron and its kinds, the hoopoe and the bat.

> The Bible states, "These you may eat, whatever is in the water: all that have fins and scales, those in the water, in the seas and in the rivers, you may eat. But whatever is in the seas and in the rivers that does not have fins and scales among all the teeming life in the water, and among all the living creatures that are in the water, they are detestable things to you, and they shall be abhorrent to you; you may not eat of their flesh, and their carcasses you shall detest. Whatever in the water does not have fins and scales is abhorrent to you" (Lev. 11:9-12).

> "Moreover, you will be made unclean whoever touches their carcasses becomes unclean until evening and

whoever picks up any of their carcasses shall wash his clothes and be unclean until evening. Concerning all the animals which divide the hoof but do not make a split hoof, or which do not chew cud, they are unclean to you; whoever touches them becomes unclean. Also, whatever walks on its paws, among all the creatures that walk on all fours, are unclean to you" (Lev. 11:24,26,27).

"Now these are to you the unclean among the swarming things which swarm on the earth: the mole, and the mouse, and the great lizard and its kinds, and gecko, and the crocodile, and the lizard, and the sand reptile, and the chameleon. Also anything on which one of them may fall when they are dead becomes unclean, including any wooden article, or clothing, or a skin, or a sack—any article of which use is made—it shall be put in the water and be unclean until evening then it becomes clean" (Lev.11:29,30,32).

"Now every swarming thing that swarms on the earth is detestable, not to be eaten. Whatever crawls on its belly, and whatever walks on all fours, whatever has many feet in respect to every swarming thing that swarms on the earth you shall not eat them, for they are detestable. Do not render yourselves detestable through any of the swarming things that swarm; and you shall not make yourselves unclean with them so that you become unclean. For I am the Lord your God. Consecrate yourselves therefore, and be holy, for I am holy. And you shall not make yourselves unclean with any of the swarming things that swarm on the earth. For I am the Lord who brought you up from the land of Egypt to be your God; thus you shall be holy, for I am holy" (Lev. 11:41-45).

"This is the law regarding the animal and the bird, and every living thing that moves in the waters and everything that swarms on the earth, to make a distinction between the unclean and the clean and between the edible creature and the creature which is not to be eaten" (Lev. 11:46-47).

As you can see the dietary laws were very strict back in the day, under the Old Covenant of Law. However, these strict laws about diet are totally reversed and made obsolete in the Book of Acts, under the New Covenant of Grace. Here are verses of scripture to support my claim, found in Acts chapter 10; "Peter went up on the housetop about the sixth hour to pray. But he became hungry and was desiring to eat; but while they were making preparations, he fell into a trance; and he saw the sky opened up, and an object like a great sheet coming down, lowered by four corners to the ground, and there were in it all kinds of four-footed animals and crawling creatures of the earth and birds of the air. A voice came to him, "Get up, Peter, *kill and eat*!" But Peter said, "By no means, Lord, for I have never eaten anything unholy and unclean." Again, a voice came to him a second time, "*What God has cleansed*, no longer consider unholy." This happened three times, and immediately the object was taken up into the sky. (Acts 10:9-16).

As you can see in the book of Acts, after the crucifixion not only did the shed blood of Jesus pay for the sin of the world, but it also cleansed and made all the insects, fish, birds and animals which had previously been called detestable, clean and holy. The death of Jesus totally reversed and made obsolete what was said in the book of Leviticus in the Old Covenant about these creatures being unclean and unholy. Here is another example that supports my findings that God's word is always true—at the time it was given. New Covenant Grace **supercedes** Old Covenant Law which has now become obsolete to the New Covenant _believer_.

Before the fall of man—when Adam and Eve sinned against God by eating the fruit of the tree of the knowledge of good and evil, which God had forbidden them to do. **All** the creatures God had created were good for mankind to eat as mentioned in Genesis chapter 1 starting on the first page of the Bible. Then God said, "Behold, I have given you every plant yielding seed that is on the surface of all the earth, and every tree which has fruit yielding seed; it shall be food for you; and to every beast of the earth and to every bird of the sky and to everything that moves on the earth which has life, I have given every green plant for food; and it was so. God saw all that he had made, and behold, *it was very good*" (Gen. 1:29-31).

Before God created man, He created all the plants and animals for him to eat and said that they were *all good to eat*. Then after Adam and Eve sinned by disobeying God, a curse was put on them and on the ground. Creatures which had previously been called good for food were now considered unclean or unholy by God and were forbidden to be eaten. Jesus was the second Adam, doing what the first Adam could not do— keep Gods laws and commandments! Jesus by living a sinless life and dying in our place to pay for our failure to keep God's commandments, redeemed us from the curse of the Law.

In the Word of God it states that the Lord gave us plants and animals for food, and He said that it was very good. Scripture says, that God gave mankind, "rule over all the fish of the sea and over the birds of the sky and over the cattle and over all the earth, and over every creeping thing that creeps on the earth" (Gen. 1:26). We have *dominion* over all the animal kingdom but we must take our responsibility seriously, and be good stewards of what God has given us by trying to preserve as many species as possible in order that future generations can enjoy what God has provided. The natural world contains about 8 million different species of creatures on this planet presently. Some scientists say that hundreds of species of insects, birds, plants, and animals become extinct every day. Hopefully, mankind will wake up and stop this trend before we and our descendants no longer have any food to eat.

CHAPTER 10

JUDGEMENT DAY vs REWARDS DAY

There are two different types of **Judgement Day** listed in the Bible; one for the unbelievers and one for believers. At the Great White Throne Judgement, which is after Armageddon and the thousand-year millennial reign of King Jesus on the earth. The Bible says the sheep will be separated from the goats (the goats are the unbelievers). The *unbelievers* will be thrown "into the eternal fire which has been prepared for the devil and his angels" (Matt. 25:41).

"And I saw the dead, the great and the small, standing before the throne (of Jesus), and books were opened; and another book was opened, which is the **Book of Life**; and the dead were judged from the things that were written in the books, according to their deeds. And the sea gave up the dead which were in it, and death and Hades gave up the dead which were in them; and they were judged, every one of them *according to their deeds*" Rev. 20:12-14). Notice it didn't say *according to their sins*. Remember, in John 3:16 Jesus said that they were *already judged* because of their unbelief. I'm of the opinion that everyone's name (*everyone who has ever lived/been given the gift of life)* is written in the *book of life*, yet if they **reject Jesus** during their time here on earth, their name will be *removed* from the book. "Then death and Hades were thrown into the lake of fire. And if anyone's name was not found written in the book of life he was thrown into the lake of fire" (Rev. 20:15). "**He who overcomes** will thus be clothed in white garments; and **_I will not erase his name from the book of life_**, and I will confess his name before My Father and before His angels" (Rev. 3:5). Jesus said, "These things I have spoken to you, so that **in Me** you may have peace. In the world you have tribulation but take courage; I have **overcome the world**" (John 16:33).

_In Me_ means **in Christ**, and if you are a believer you are _in Christ_. And The **overcomer** dwells in you in the person of His Holy Spirit! Christians are the ones who are called '**He who overcomes**'.

There will be a different judgment for _believers_ called the judgement seat of Christ. "For we must all appear before the judgment seat of Christ, so that each one may be **_recompensed_** (not judged) for his deeds in the body, according to what he has done, whether good or bad" (2 Cor. 5:10). Notice it didn't say judged for his deeds, it says recompensed (rewarded) for his deeds. The Greek language uses the word judge in two different senses, one for condemnation and one for the giving of rewards. The Bible says the unbelievers will be *condemned* while the believers will be *rewarded*. At the judgement seat of Christ another book will be opened, called the **Lambs Book of Life**. Every person who had faith and believed in Jesus has their name recorded in it.

The Bible gives a description of the believers Judgement day;

> "According to the grace of God which was given to me, like a wise master builder I laid a foundation, and another is building on it. But each man must be careful how he builds on it. For no man can lay a foundation other than the one which is laid, which is Jesus Christ. Now if any man builds on the foundation with gold, silver, precious stones, wood, hay, straw, each man's work will become evident; for the day will show it because it is to be revealed with fire, and the fire itself will test the quality of each man's work. If any man's work which he has built on it remains, he will receive a **reward**. If any

man's work is burned up, he will suffer
loss; but he himself **WILL BE SAVED**, yet
so as through fire" (1 Cor. 3:10-15).

As you can see, here it says that even if the believers
work is burned up (dead works), he or she will *still be*
saved! **The good works** (the works that will remain)
are symbolized by the words *gold*, *silver*, and *precious*
stones. And the **dead works** (works that will be burned
up) are symbolized by the words *wood*, *hay*, and *straw*.
Those building on the foundation of Jesus Christ are
the born-again. They will be (*rewarded/recompensed*)
for their good works. However, any dead works committed by the born-again believer will be burned up, and
they will suffer loss, but they *will be saved* (**Eternal Life**
anyone)? Here's more evidence supporting the com-
ment I made earlier that *good works do not save you*
and *bad works do not send you to hell*. Because Jesus
paid for your bad works (sin), sin has been taken out of
the picture as far as salvation is concerned. It's only by
being born-again through faith in Jesus Christ that you
can be saved.

Jesus said "I am the true vine, and my Father is the
vinedresser. Every branch in Me that does not bear fruit,

He takes away; and every branch that bears fruit, He prunes it so that it may bear more fruit. I am the vine, you are the branches; he who abides in Me and I in him, he bears much fruit, for apart from me you can do nothing. If anyone does not abide in Me, he is thrown away as a branch and dries up; and they gather them and cast them into the fire and they are **_burned_**" (John 15:1,5,6). Here, there is more clarity about what Jesus meant by the term _abide in Me_, "Whoever _confesses that Jesus is the Son of God_, **God abides in him**, and he in God. God is love, and the one who **_abides in love_** abides in God, and God abides in him. By this, love is perfected with us, so that we may have confidence in the **Day of Judgement**; because as He is, so are we in this world. There is no fear in love; but perfect love casts out fear, because fear involves punishment, and the one who fears is not perfected in love. We love, because He first loved us" (1 John 4:15-19). "These things I have written to you who **_believe_** in the name of the Son of God, so that **_you may know that you have eternal life_**" (1 John 5:13).

CHAPTER 11

CONCLUSION

J esus said **be not afraid**, **don't worry**, **fear not**, and **be anxious for nothing**, at different times in the scriptures. As He was sitting on the Mount of Olives, the disciples came to Him privately, saying, "Tell us, when will these things happen, and what will be the sign of Your coming, and of the **end of the age**?" And Jesus answered and said to them, "See to it that no one misleads you. For many will come in My name, saying, 'I am the Christ,' and will mislead many. You will be hearing of **wars and rumors of wars**. See that **you are not frightened**, for those things must take place, but that is not yet the end. For nation will rise against nation, and kingdom against kingdom, and in various places there will be **famines** and **earthquakes**. But all these things are merely the beginning of birth pangs. Then they will deliver you to tribulation, and will kill you, and you will be hated by all nations because of My name. At that time many will fall away and will betray one another. Many false prophets will arise and will mislead many. Because **lawlessness is increased**, most people's **love will grow cold**. But the one who endures to the end, he will be saved. This gospel of the kingdom shall be preached in the whole world as a testimony to all the nations, and then the end will come." (Matt. 24:4-14)

With the invention of radio, television, the computer, the internet, satellites, social media etc., it's more likely now than at any other time in the history of earth, that the gospel can actually reach the whole world as Jesus prophesied in Matthew chapter 24. As I was writing the last few chapters of this book the world began experiencing the covid-19 pandemic. At the time of this writing It's being said that over 200,000 people have died from this virus in the United States alone. Jesus said in the Book of Luke, "and there will be **great earthquakes**, and in various places **plagues** and **famines**; and there will be **terrors** and **great signs** from heaven." (Luke 21:11).

These are very trying times in which we live, with millions of people out of work and so many businesses closing their doors, it's causing great uncertainty about the future. On television, we see people sitting in their cars for hours in lines that are several miles long hoping to get some food. People rioting in the down-town streets of our major cities chanting overthrow cap-italism and defund the police! Tearing down statues of our founding fathers and trying to destroy our national monuments. It's as if we are seeing prophecy being ful-filled right before our very eyes with all the earthquakes, wars, rumors of war, plagues and famine. While ***unbe-lievers are fearful*** and asking, what's the meaning of all this? Believers know that Lord Jesus is about to return for the **rapture** of the church, and we are excited and looking forward to it! We have hope but the unbelievers don't, and that's why they are so discontent, depressed, and angry!

In this book I have attempted to help you *find the truth* about the *New Covenant*. And to show you how many modern-day preachers are capitalizing and deceiving the masses with many false teachings. For many years now, they have been deceiving us about forgiveness, salvation, giving, diet, and Judgement Day. I hope these teachings have been helpful to you in your search for ***truth***. "Beloved, I pray that in all respects you may prosper and be in good health, just as your soul prospers" (3 John 1:2). May Abba Father greatly *reward you* for diligently seeking Him. And may He ***bless you*** abundantly for seeking the **truth** about His New Covenant in Christ Jesus. "For God so loved the *world*, that He gave His only begotten Son, that whosoever believes in Him shall not perish but have eternal life" (John 3:16). "But when these things begin to take place, straighten up and lift up your heads, because your redemption is drawing near" (Luke 21:28). Amen

Averialo3337@gmail.com or retrain013@gmail.com